babies'ROOMS
from zero to three

babies'ROOMS

from zero to three

JUDITH WILSON   photography by WINFRIED HEINZE

RYLAND

PETERS

& SMALL

LONDON NEW YORK

Designer **Pamela Daniels**
Commissioning editor **Annabel Morgan**
Location research **Tracy Ogino**
Production manager **Patricia Harrington**
Art director **Anne-Marie Bulat**
Editorial director **Julia Charles**
Publishing director **Alison Starling**

First published in the United Kingdom in
2006 by Ryland Peters & Small
20–21 Jockey's Fields
London WC1R 4BW
www.rylandpeters.com

10 9 8 7 6 5 4 3 2 1

ISBN-10: 1 84597 145 0
ISBN-13: 978 1 84597 145 8

A CIP record for this book is available
from the British Library.

Printed and bound in China.

contents

INTRODUCTION

The arrival of a new baby is a major milestone. Your personal life will never be quite the same again, nor, from the moment that first teddy lands on the sofa, will the life of your home. It's vital to accept that now. But if you are able to plan for baby's new existence, using a practical eye and a sense of fun, the transition from child-free zone to dynamic family home can be seamless.

Whether you're expecting newborn number one or the arrival of a sibling, space at home – or the lack of it – is a crucial issue. It can be tempting to move house, but is that disruption really essential? It is often better to wait until you have some first-hand experience of life with a baby (or even a couple of youngsters), so you can work out exactly what constitutes your ideal living space.

Choosing equipment (and working out where it all goes) is equally pressing. Try to ignore the exhaustive

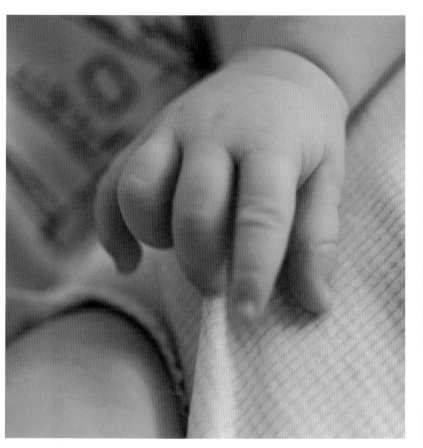 

list of kit baby shops would like you to buy. Babies have very basic needs – somewhere to sleep, a changing zone and a place to play – so focus only on essential equipment in the early days. For many parents, the arrival of a baby means a drop in income, so try not to waste money on things that will quickly become redundant.

Remember that, while creating a cosy nursery bedroom for your baby is a natural, fulfilling task (and the really fun part!), minor adjustments will be needed everywhere. You'll

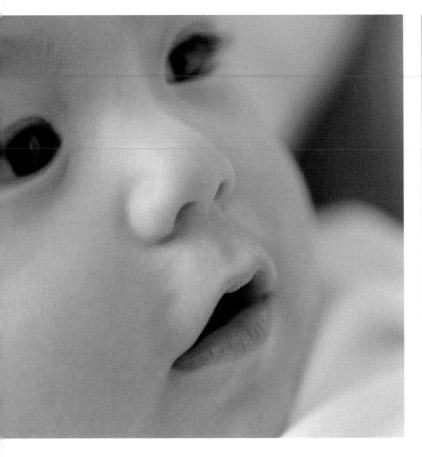

want more storage, not to mention making space in the bathroom, the kitchen and your bedroom for the new incumbent to share. Surfaces everywhere need to be practical, and – as baby becomes mobile – potential danger zones must be made safe.

Thankfully, it is possible to have a baby-friendly house that retains its stylish good looks. There has been a boom in well-designed kids' furniture and accessories, so whether you want cutting-edge chic or a nostalgic mood there will be something to suit. Enjoy

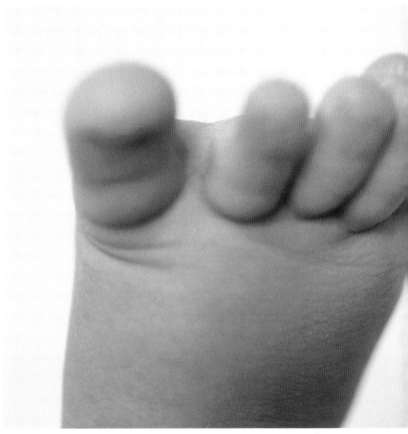

researching good-looking kit and integrating it into your home.

Above all, remember that from day one your home needs to adapt as your little one grows and as new siblings arrive. Babies develop with alarming speed. In zero to three years, tinies go from kicking on a mat to scooting around a playroom, from the security of a swinging crib to the maturity of a full-size bed. Anticipate their needs, stay true to your style and turn a blind eye to a little bit of chaos. Welcome to family living!

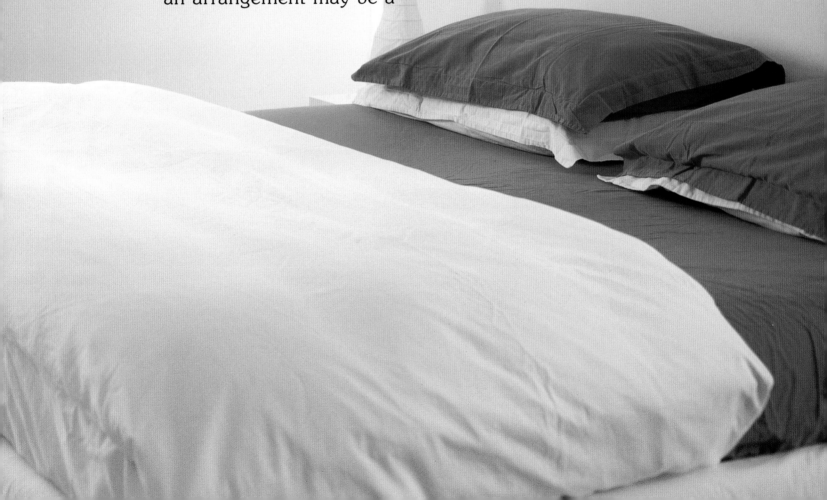

Many parents prefer to keep a newborn in their own bedroom in the early days. For couples without a spare bedroom for a nursery, or those living in an open-plan apartment, such an arrangement may be a necessity. Plan your space carefully, to ensure that baby has a quiet nook of its very own and so you don't feel too invaded by the new arrival.

this page **If baby is sleeping in your room, the lighting may need some subtle changes. Add a dimmer switch to overhead lights, so you don't have to get undressed in the dark, and fit lower-wattage bulbs to bedside lamps, so you can read in bed without disturbing baby.**

Streamline the contents of your bedside table. There should be space for muslin squares, nappies and a glass of water for you if you're breast-feeding.

opposite, top right
Allocate a special place for soft toys, so they don't take over the entire bedroom.

Flowers or a scented candle will provide a gentle ambience for you and baby.

Few of us are truly prepared for the reality of a new baby. We may buy all the kit, and read the books, but the reality of a newborn – the crying, the feeding, the changing – is often a shock, not to mention the accompanying sleep deprivation. If you add to that mix limited time for organizing, perhaps the demands of toddler siblings, and heightened emotions all round, it's not surprising things can get a little fraught.

If you have chosen to keep your baby in your bedroom, even just for a few weeks, do plan carefully to ensure that your once-peaceful zone doesn't suffer too much disruption. The advantages of having the baby close to you are manifold: you won't need to go to another room to feed or change, you can keep a watchful eye on your little one, and a baby derives great comfort from sharing a room with its parents.

When planning, consider the best position for the Moses basket or cot. In the early days, you'll want it beside the bed. Is there also room for extras, such as a breast-feeding pillow? Even if you have furnished a separate nursery for baby, it is worth keeping essentials in your room to avoid having to trek across the landing at night. A changing mat, for example, can be discreetly tucked under the bed, with toiletries for nappy changes stacked on a mobile trolley. Spare sleepsuits can be piled into a wicker basket, or you could clear a space in your own chest of drawers.

below **Grown-up window treatments, such as unlined curtains, will need to be adapted so that the room can be kept dark for daytime naps. Add a plain white blackout roller blind, or swap sheers for thicker lined curtains.**

Display your personal
selection of baby pictures in
conventional frames, or
order a canvas printed with
a favourite digital image.

this page **Provided you keep things neatly folded, everything from sleepsuits to nappy changing toiletries look good in wicker baskets with a fabric lining. An open-topped basket allows easy access.**

opposite, left **If baby is in your bedroom long-term, convert one section of your wardrobe into a changing area. Add a mat on top of a chest of drawers, with space for a nappy disposal system.**

left **Invest in smart-looking metal, cardboard or wicker storage boxes, which can be stacked on existing shelves to keep baby's things tidy.**

Do give due consideration to the decorative impact of the baby's bed. It certainly eases the shock of having a new incumbent if the crib harmonizes with the scheme in your bedroom. If you have blond wood detailing, choose a cot with bleached tones or in white, or if the look is modern pick a funky oval design. You can choose baby blankets and a cot bumper to match the existing colour scheme. Save pattern or strong contrasts for when baby moves into his or her own room.

If space permits, it's a good idea to add an armchair or even a small sofa to the master bedroom. This provides a comfortable, tranquil spot for feeding baby during the day, or a good place for you to cuddle up with a small sibling. Brothers or sisters may feel jealous if a new baby takes root in their parents' bedroom. If children make a habit of night visits, it will make everyone's lives easier if you provide a soft mattress and a blanket on the other side of your bed, so they have a special place to settle in your room, too.

Do remember that, as well as creating a peaceful sleeping zone for your new baby, your bedroom must continue to provide you and your partner with respite. Treat yourself to a favourite scented candle, a new set of bed linen and a comforting wool throw to wrap around yourself if you're up feeding baby in the night.

THE UNISEX NURSERY

Keep your plans simple for a first nursery, especially if decorating prior to the baby's birth. Concentrate on choosing the right basics, which can be added to as time goes by. If you don't know your baby's sex, there's no point fretting over pinks and blues. Think outside the box: unisex colour schemes, from all white to apple, tangerine or cherry, make a refreshing change.

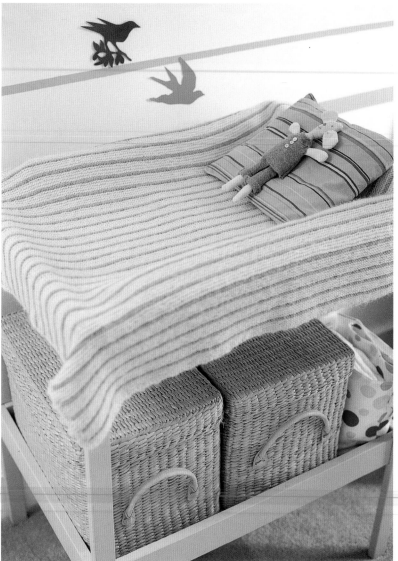

Stylized bird and flower motifs make a change from teddies.

When planning a first nursery, it's very tempting to start by plunging in and selecting a colour scheme or choosing the furniture. Yet what matters more is allocating the right room for your baby. Often there's no choice: a first child goes into the only spare bedroom available. But if there are options, the ideal location is next door to your bedroom, or at the very least on the same floor, so you can hear crying and don't have to walk far in the night. Try to avoid placing the nursery

opposite, left **A washable blanket and soft pillow make a warm and cosy alternative to a wipe-clean vinyl changing mat. While you are changing nappies, keep baby amused with an overhead mobile, a brightly stencilled motif, or soft toys to hand.**

this picture **If you want to display toys from your own childhood, or books not yet suitable for baby, group them attractively out of reach.**
right **Jazz up plain white paintwork by cutting out bird, butterfly or flower shapes and sticking them to the walls.**

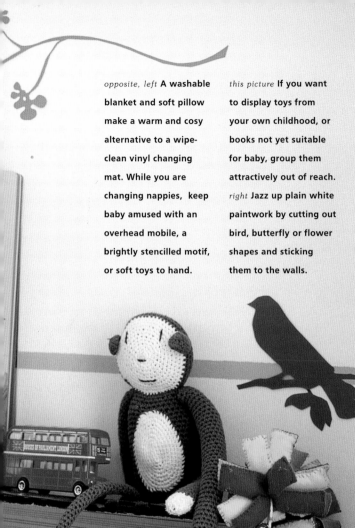

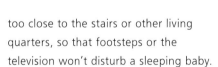

too close to the stairs or other living quarters, so that footsteps or the television won't disturb a sleeping baby.

If you already have one child, there are some choices to be made. If he or she occupies the former spare room, consider a loft extension, which can be more cost-effective than moving house. If an older sibling is already in the 'baby' room next to yours, and there's a larger bedroom elsewhere, it may be the right time to promote a toddler to greater independence.

But if jealousy is likely, don't move the older child. Instead, convert an upstairs study or dressing room into a tiny nursery. A boxroom or attic conversion makes a cosy first room.

Whether you are just redecorating the baby's room or doing up a whole house, consider practicalities like the lighting and other services now. You will need to control the level of electric light, so fit a dimmer switch to overhead lights. The addition of wall lights close to the cot will do away with the need for a bedside light. Do you have enough power points? As well as a baby monitor, a CD player for music and a fan in summer, you may wish to plug in a nightlight. Anticipate safety needs now, and buy socket covers for all unused power

Cater for the possibility of a baby girl or boy by choosing a predominantly white scheme, accented with pastel pinks and blues, and a classic mix of stripes and florals.

this page **An attic bedroom, with its sloping ceilings, makes a cosy choice for a new baby. Furnish it simply, with an armchair, a cot and a chest of drawers. Ensure that an attic room has a decent-sized window, as well as a fan, so baby doesn't get overheated in summer.** *opposite* **Tongue and groove panelling is a crisp-looking, easy-care alternative to painted walls or wallpaper.**

Hand-made accessories add instant personality to a new baby's bedroom.

points. Check that both heating and ventilation are adequate: a steady temperature of 18°C is ideal.

Most new parents will be kitting out a nursery from scratch, and just purchasing the basics – the cot, some storage, a chair – can be something of an investment. It's tempting to buy an entire set of matching furniture, but it really isn't essential. All too soon, a toddler will outgrow scaled-down pieces, and you'll have to start all over again. If you are set on the coordinated look, seek out ranges that are specifically designed to grow up with the child, such as those with a full-height wardrobe, or a matching first bed. Buy all the pieces at the same time, as some nursery ranges are discontinued with alarming speed.

You'll achieve a more personal-looking nursery, however, if you mix grown-up pieces of furniture, such as a chest of drawers and a trunk, with an attractive cot. Make the cot your first major buy. Happily, the days of the ubiquitous pine cot have gone. There are many beautifully designed styles on the market, across all price ranges, from wrought-iron styles to classic woods like oak, maple and

beech. If you don't yet know the sex of your baby, pick a classic style in plain wood or white.

Spend some time in a nursery showroom investigating the practicalities. Ideally, a cot should have three base positions and a one- or two-hand drop-side mechanism. Castors are also useful. It's personal choice whether you go for a cot or a cotbed. If you've just started a family, then it's cost-effective to buy one good cot, which can be used by each successive baby as older siblings move on to a single bed. On the other hand, a cotbed gives a growing toddler emotional security, as it transfers from cot to bed. A cot will last a baby until two years old, whereas a cotbed, with its sides removed, will last up to five years.

You will also need an efficient nappy changing area, but don't feel under pressure to buy a changing table. It will be soon be redundant (though some styles are designed to convert into a toy storage unit). Either put a changing mat on top of a chest of drawers (using the top drawers for essentials like nappies, creams and wipes), or look out for a small table

this page **Choose furniture that sits well with the architecture of your home. In this nursery, the pale weatherboarded furniture blends sympathetically with the ceiling beams, while providing much-needed relief from the dark wood. Look for matching sets that will grow up with baby: for example, once the mat is removed,** **this changing unit will become a toy cupboard.**

opposite above **In a small room, plan the layout with care. By projecting this cot diagonally, the parents have access to both sides and the room feels less poky.**

opposite below left and right **In a dark bedroom, jolly, brightly coloured accessories will lift the mood and are suitable for both sexes.**

with a shelf underneath. If you're decorating a baby's room from scratch, you could have a custom-made changing zone built. Some cots come with a cot-top changer, which slots over the top of the cot and saves space in a small nursery.

In the early days there's no need for lots of storage. Of course, if you're doing a nursery from scratch, a built-in wardrobe or free-standing armoire is ideal, long-term. Otherwise, you can get away with a capacious chest of drawers, which can hold everything from spare bedding to clothes, or an open shelf unit stacked with wicker baskets. Combine closed storage with peg rails – great for little hats and hooded towels. Baskets or rubber tubs are perfect for soft toys and books. And a wicker or plastic laundry bin will see your child through to adulthood.

An armchair is a must, for feeding and reading bedtime stories. Any comfortable chair will do; you don't have to buy a special feeding chair. Look for a low-slung style, with good lumbar support, and low arms that won't get in the way if you're breast-feeding. Choose sensible upholstery.

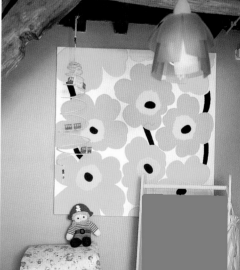

Have a loose cover made in washable cotton or denim or, in a modern room, a leather chair, which will wipe clean. If there are toddler siblings, add a bean bag or soft seating cubes, so they can join in.

For a first nursery, keep things simple in decorative terms. There is plenty of time, in later years, to personalize a small child's bedroom. So stick to plain furnishings, and avoid fussy details. Painted walls, a neutral carpet or painted floorboards, and full-length curtains in plain cotton, or a blind, are ideal.

Order blinds with a blackout lining, or buy ready-made blackout curtain linings to fit existing drapes.

In the first year at least, it is you – rather than your baby – who will take pleasure from the decorative scheme. An all-white combination is tranquil, and looks good with pastel or bright accessories. If you want to use colour, then one wall painted in a clear bright shade, such as apple green or coral, looks fresh and pretty. Gentle pattern, in the form of gingham curtains, or an animal-print floor cushion, adds character without dominating.

opposite, left **In a small room, built-in storage will free up floor space and looks smart and modern. This clever changing station has shelves above for muslins and creams, and cupboards below for stacking bulkier items like spare nappies. In later years, the shelves can hold books and toys.** *opposite, right* **Having a baby doesn't have to mean sacrificing style: a classic Eames chair will be comforting for rocking baby to sleep.** *this page* **Choose open shelves for storing baby kit that is in daily use, so you can access nappies or toiletries with one hand.**

A monochromatic scheme provides a soothing blank canvas for a new baby and its first possessions.

this page **Choose practical and soft nursery flooring, as tinies will spend lots of time crawling and playing on the floor. A wool carpet is better than fibres such as sisal or coir, which can be too rough for delicate skin and don't clean well. If you've gone** for a monochromatic scheme, with colour splashes from toys and accessories, it's safer to pick a plain carpet, such as dove grey or biscuit. A close pile provides a satisfyingly flat surface that's ideal for balancing toys on the floor.

Plain, painted white walls allow you the freedom to decorate using your growing baby's artwork, with all its colourful, naive appeal.

The best way to add personality is by choosing decorative cot bedding. There is a huge choice of fun, colourful accessories. Steer clear of a fully coordinated set (and be aware that babies under 12 months must not use a pillow or a baby duvet), and mix and match. Good choices include an appliquéd cotton quilt, a brightly coloured fleece blanket and perhaps a gingham or striped cotton bumper.

Don't overload a new baby's room with too many accessories. A baby is just as happy watching dancing sunbeams as a carefully executed painting, and it takes time to fill up a new little person's room with their own special things. Add a shelf to show off cute toys and christening gifts. These days there's an increasing vogue for personalized gifts for babies. A painted wooden initial, a cot blanket embroidered with baby's birth date, or even a toy from your own childhood, will all provide an excellent starting point.

ROOMS FOR GIRLS

Pink is the ultimate colour choice for girls and, with such a range of attractive hues, from shell to raspberry, it gives you the flexibility to go traditional or modern. Clear, bright shades, from acid yellow to turquoise, can look equally pretty. Design your baby girl's room to evolve with her, so concentrate on combining grown-up feminine touches with a sense of fun.

A plain white mat and a wicker
basket to hold nappies creates
a discreet changing zone.

opposite, right **A grown-up chest of drawers, repainted in white, cream or a sugared almond shade, can double up as a changing table. Deep drawers hold clothing, spare bedding and baby toiletries.**

below right **This attic bedroom is girly without being twee. The simple white furniture and the American-style shutters counteract the sweetness of the pale pink painted walls.**

right **A small shelf, positioned out of your baby's grasp, is a good place to display christening treasures and classic books.**

Whether you're decorating for a little girl on the way, or planning a nursery for a baby girl graduating from her Moses basket, knowing the sex of your baby makes a difference. However politically correct we may wish to be, few of us can resist colour-coding. Our grown-up fashion and design tastes may be cool and trendy, but it's hard to resist the charm of little girls' pink accessories.

The secret, of course, is to steer a tasteful course through the lurid pink and fairy-emblazoned merchandise in the shops, and devise a subtle yet charming decorative scheme. Whether you go traditional, chic or modern is down to your personal style. But remember that your little girl's room should harmonize with the rest of the décor at home. If the look elsewhere is elegant, with linen curtains and dark wood floors, take this as your starting point and lighten the scheme using sugared almond

below **Simple window treatments can be dressed up with a decorative curtain pole, such as this barley-twist design, or choose a modern metal pole with a colourful glass ball or flower-motif finial.**

right **For a baby girl's nursery, a flower-print wallpaper looks** irresistibly pretty. Pick a decent-size motif, as tiny sprigs can look indistinct on the walls. For a retro look, opt for a gently faded design.

opposite, left **Much-loved family treasures, such as a rocking horse or a cross-stitch sampler, add instant personality to a little girl's bedroom.**

colours and satin ribbon detailing. In a trendy household, with retro 20th-century furniture, incorporate a piece in the nursery, and use vintage fabrics for curtains.

On the birth of a first child, it may seem that the baby stage will go on forever. But very quickly that baby turns into a toddler and then a little girl with definite opinions. So plan with an eye on the future, and add flexibility to your scheme. You may love Cinderella-style bedroom furniture, but a tomboy two-year-old may not approve. Equally, a modern built-in nursery in muted colours can look quite bizarre filled with fluffy pink accessories. So try not to be too extreme in your design choices.

Choose key pieces in a classic design; then, as years go by, you can change the look of the room using new paint colours, wallpaper and bedding.

The cot is the inevitable focus in a little girl's bedroom. If you're buying for a first-born daughter, and think the cot may be needed for a boy later, look for pretty, yet not overtly girly detailing. Scroll carving, scalloped contours or elegantly curved ends on the head- and foot-boards are all appropriate. If you're buying a cot-bed for your daughter to use until she's five, you can adopt a more feminine look. A sleigh-bed style or a wooden cotbed with simple heart or star cut-out detailing will please a growing toddler without

top and above **Little girls don't really need a huge wardrobe (save that for later years!) and their clothes are so adorable they deserve to be on display. Hang little dresses from door hooks, hat-stands and painted wooden peg rails.**

For a contemporary spin on the classic girl's colour scheme, combine bright lipstick-pink with bold shades like scarlet, graphite and apple green.

right **When planning a scheme, do take into account any dominant architectural features. This loft apartment, with its high ceilings and large windows, required strong blocks of colour and bold modern motifs to balance the outsize proportions. Comforting textures, from the dense carpet pile to the floppy, fleecy floor cushions, make it cosy for a toddler. While it's fun for a little one to have lots of floor space to play on, in a big room ensure that the cot is placed against one wall so that the child feels a sense of enclosure and safety.**

looking twee. If you're stuck with a very plain cot, then a mosquito net or gingham canopy adds a pretty touch.

Once your baby girl gets beyond the cot stage, you have choices. For little ones that crave security, what are often termed 'first beds' are ideal. Designed to grow with your toddler, they can be extended in sections, and are close to the ground. Some even come with an integral bed guard. For a traditional look, choose a high-sided style, with classic detailing or, for a more contemporary finish, a slatted head- and foot-board.

If you have a child who is happy to go straight into a bed, invest in a 2'6" or 3' single to last her up to her teens. Look for a classic style that will grow with her, like an upholstered divan (which can be updated with new fabric in later years), an antique-style wrought-iron bed, or a modern bed with under-bed storage. Long before baby graduates from her cot, you can place the bed in the room. It will provide somewhere for you to sleep during a disturbed night, and your little one can slowly get used to the idea of a grown-up bed.

above **Adding a tiny play table and chairs to a nursery makes life more interesting for babies just learning to walk, and is a cosy place for toddlers to draw or give a dolly's tea party.**

left **Abstract prints, in jolly primary colours, make a bright splash on plain white walls.**

Baby girls can enjoy elegance, too!

Enjoy dressing up your baby's cot or bed with attractive linens, but don't overload it: most children don't like too many bedclothes. For a baby, the basics are a fitted cot sheet and cotton cellular blankets. A first bed might need a pillow, duvet, scatter cushions and a quilt or blanket on top. The colours and patterns you choose will affect the overall look of the room, particularly if the rest of the decoration is simple. If you've gone for a cool white scheme, add a girly touch using strong pastel plains in shades like grass or lilac. For a classic finish, a decorative quilt, featuring patchwork, appliqué or

opposite, above and below **A low, wide console table, teamed with a stool, makes a sensible choice for a changing table. This beautiful combination, teaming chic wood with snakeskin upholstery, is the perfect example of long-term planning, as when baby grows up the table will become a dressing table for her.**

below, centre **Positioned suitably low over the cot, and fitted with a dimmer switch, a wall light gives a comforting glow at night and can't be knocked over by a busy toddler.**

this page **A pillow bearing baby's birth date and full name or a monogrammed cushion deserves pride of place in any little girl's room.**

embroidery provides warmth and may come with a matching cot bumper. Detailing like ric-rac braid, scalloped edges and monograms look both pretty and chic.

While it's fun to add pattern using bedding (and these days the sky's the limit on motifs, from cupcakes and fairies to hearts and flowers), do try to avoid using a fully coordinated range with matching quilt, curtains and lampshade. Your aim is to personalize the room, not make it look like a room set. Using pattern on the walls sets a particularly dominant theme. Traditional floral wallpaper looks prettily nostalgic, while bold, stylized flowers would suit a

Bright, energizing shades are as appealing for little girls as traditional pink, and make a great background for primary-coloured toys.

above, left and centre **A** bedroom should be a peaceful zone to sleep in, but there must still be things to look at. While a baby will enjoy a mobile, toddlers relish ceiling-hung attractions such as wooden birds, paper dragons and papier mâché 'makes'. Add plenty of shelves for bedtime books.

left and this page **Getting the scale right in the bedroom goes a long way towards creating a cosy atmosphere for little people. This bedroom, tucked beneath a mezzanine floor in a double-height city apartment, has been** tailor-made to suit its small owner. The little bed is close to the ground, as are the open shelves, making it easy to access toys. The touch-catch mechanism on the doors of the large storage unit keeps grown-up things out of her grasp.

this page **This offbeat yet elegant baby girl's room proves you don't have to sacrifice style for family life. Later on, the chest of drawers and chic lighting could be moved to a sitting room, or incorporated into an older girl's bedroom. Have fun customizing the odd piece for your nursery. Here, the rug bears the initial of the little girl, and an armchair is scaled down to suit a toddler.**

opposite **Brighten an essentially simple decorative scheme with subtle, pretty detailing, such as a hand-painted cot panel and a bold pelmet design.**

contemporary interior. A hand-painted border, in a pastel colour, sits well with white-washed furniture and a modern-country mood.

If you don't want to use pattern, it's still possible to set an unusual decorative tone with colour. Pink isn't mandatory, but it does have its advantages – it's easy on the eye, most little (and big) girls love it, and you can interpret it across a vast range. Steer clear of traditional pale pinks, and look at a paint chart to remind yourself of the many variations. For the trendiest take,

choose one candy-floss painted wall, teamed with lilac, which looks great with dark wood furniture. For a moodier slant (and an excellent accompaniment to hand-painted pieces), choose pale grey for walls, with raspberry upholstery. But don't be a slave to pink if it doesn't appeal. You can still achieve a pretty girl's room using brights like leaf green, egg-yolk yellow or scarlet.

Unless you're after a very pared-down modern look (in which case, roller blinds or shutters are ideal), a girl's room offers the opportunity

below If you don't want to opt for traditional floral or gingham fabrics, then abstract motifs like circles or hearts make a very jolly alternative.

right For a bedroom that will evolve tastefully as your daughter grows from a baby into a little girl, choose simple white walls, a wooden floor, and white or wooden furniture. It is a child's ever-increasing selection of possessions, from framed prints to quirky chairs, that will add a sense of personality and vibrancy of colour.

Framed baby close-ups add personality to a nursery.

above **Tucked into the corner, with a softly upholstered headboard, this cosy bed will be welcoming for a two-year-old, but will also be suitable for an older child, too. An upholstery fabric in a bright pastel shade coordinates easily with most patterned bed linens.**

to indulge in decorative window treatments. Full-length curtains teamed with a blackout blind or fitted with a blackout lining always look pretty. Choose a simple, unfussy style – pinch pleats or tie-top headings are ideal. Stick to plains, gingham or a simple floral, rather than nursery motif material. Good curtains are expensive, and your child will outgrow baby fabrics all too quickly. Instead, dress up plain curtains with subtle detailing such as pin-tucks, a decorative pelmet or a contrast colour or ribbon border.

Every self-respecting baby girl has an ever-growing array of clothes and shoes, all of which must be stored. As well as everyday wear, there will be special-occasion dresses and hand-knitted cardies, not to mention clothes about to be grown into (or just grown out of). A chest of drawers is perfect. If you want one with feminine detail, either paint a junk-shop find in a washed-out pastel, or look for a modern one featuring a pretty scallop edge or heart cut-out detail. Glass-fronted drawers show off stacked clothes very nicely.

A built-in or free-standing wardrobe is ideal, so you can hang dresses and coats. Wicker baskets or fabric-lined boxes can be tucked into the bottom of a wardrobe to organize shoes. If there's no room for a wardrobe, a wall-mounted shelf with a peg rail beneath will allow you to display tiny shoes and her prettiest dresses. And don't forget a wall-mounted mirror, hung low down, which she will find endlessly diverting.

Don't overdo the accessories in your daughter's room, so that, as she's given treasures of her own, the room will evolve naturally. Start the collection with a few personal pieces: frame up a black-and-white baby photograph, her hand-print, and so on. And, while it's wonderful to include frivolous, girly detailing, exercise some restraint. Every little girl, from a very early age, should learn that less is always more.

above left and right **When choosing a first bed, look for styles with curved side panels that will stop a child falling out of bed. Ease a little girl into a new bed by providing cosy textures to cuddle up with. Eiderdowns, cotton quilts and soft blankets are a good choice.**

Dressing-up clothes
can look very pretty
left out on display.

above **As well as a full-height wardrobe for hanging clothes, try to incorporate as much low-level storage as possible. Built-in banquettes, with a lift-up lid, or a traditional toy chest, provide excellent storage for dressing-up clothes, soft toys and bulkier dolls' equipment, and are easily accessed.**

Have fun devising a baby boy's bedroom with a spirit of adventure or a touch of whimsy, but don't forget it must feel safe and cosy, too. Stick to solid furniture, plainly styled, and a simple layout, so busy little boys have maximum space for running about. Think beyond classic blues and add dayglo bright shades, natural textures or modern white to your palette.

ROOMS FOR BOYS

this page and opposite, left This modern little boy's bedroom proves that, without a single nursery motif in sight, you can still create a whimsical bedroom. Here, the fun comes from the primary-coloured walls, the striped rug and design-classic wall hooks, while the jolly fabric elephant hood adds a dash of fantasy. If you are design-conscious, keep the theme going in the baby's room. With their gentle curves, this table, stool and cotbed are elegant for grown-ups to look at, and safe for little ones to use.

opposite, right A changing table on castors can be moved around the nursery as necessary.

In the early months, there's little difference between putting together a baby boy's room and a baby girl's. The nursery you create for either sex should be a peaceful haven, as well as a gently stimulating place for baby to play when awake. Yet the room you plan now should cater for your son at least until he's three. During that time, he'll change from a gurgling infant to a busy little boy with very different needs. Boys aren't always rowdier than girls, but if you plan for a bit of rough and tumble in the nursery, everyone can relax.

Traditionally, boys have had something of a raw deal when it comes to bedrooms. For a start,

it's tempting to assume that tiny boys won't notice their surroundings. Yet your son has just as much right to a beautiful room as a girl, and so, as his parents, do you! Also, it can be harder for mothers (who, odds on, will be doing the scheme) to get excited about devising what they assume must be a blue room, with inevitable cars and stripes. But you don't have to stick to a conventional scheme. These days there are an increasing number of whimsical decorative ranges for tinies, from deep-sea creatures and jungle animals to city skylines, any of which will create an imaginative spring-board for a boy's room.

A pure white scheme, planned with simple shapes, is the ideal background for the inevitable collection of brightly coloured toys.

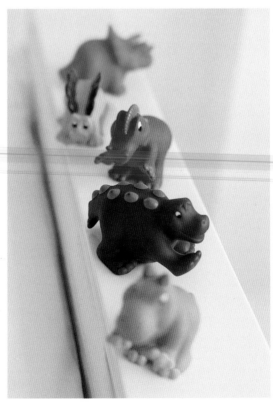

Do remember not to go too grown-up, too soon. You (or dad) may love the idea of a sports theme, with football-emblazoned bedding, or an army bedroom, with camouflage motifs. But save these for a school-age child, who will appreciate their significance (and cool factor). In the baby years, it's more fun for your little one if he can identify simple images in his bedroom, such as sailing boats and farm animals. Colours should be refreshing and clear. Boys have a lifetime of murky colours ahead, from grey school shorts to navy suits, so let them enjoy fun shades while they can.

The key nursery furniture pieces must work hard, so buy them before you devise your colour scheme.

Little ones adore mirrors, so add one to every bedroom.

opposite, left and right Usually, it's girls who are treated to a bed canopy, such as a romantic mosquito net, but little boys think it's fun, too. This safe, simple leaf design, fixed to the headboard, makes the transition from a cot to a first bed feel cosy yet exciting. In a more traditional-style room, suspend a flag, or a scaled-down canvas boat sail, above the bed.

this page Hang wall-mounted storage and accessories with small people in mind. The jolly orange mirror and shelves for teddies are low enough to be easily accessed by a little boy, which encourages early independence.

this page **A brightly coloured pattern, be it wallpaper or fabric, provides an easy decorative starting point for a nursery scheme. Here, the retro-inspired cowboy wallpaper has inspired scarlet and bright-blue accent shades. A plain wooden cot, a three-legged stool for story-time and a shelf for clothes and little possessions provide the necessary basics in a newborn boy's bedroom.**

opposite **It's fun to personalize a baby's room with special accessories. Many baby-gift mail-order catalogues offer a bespoke service, and can add names and a memorable date to anything from bed covers to cushions or a painted canvas.**

In many ways, the cot style you choose for a boy is particularly crucial, because – once you're past the tiny baby stage – you (and he) won't want it to look too pretty. Opt for the plainest cot you can find. Squared off foot- and head-ends look more restrained, as do panelled ends. Avoid a cot with cute engraved motifs, such as teddies, which may be deemed babyish by a small boy. As he moves to toddlerhood, a plain cot can be perked up with a clip-on fabric canopy in the shape of an animal head or a giant leaf.

It's a good idea to pick a wooden cot, rather than one with a pristine white-painted finish. The inevitable knocks won't show up quite so much, and wood's natural tones will work well with bright colours or more subdued tones, from blue to olive green. These days there's a good choice of wood veneers, including birch, oak and beech, as well as inexpensive pine. If you have the budget, and want something really special, some children's furniture companies will create a bespoke cot in a wood of your choice. If you prefer a painted cot, then a colour-washed tongue and groove style, or one with a distressed finish, is a good choice.

Boys love the security of their cot just as much as girls, but may want to graduate to the excitement of a full-size bed more quickly. This can pose a problem, given that a small boy may fancy the delights of a bunk bed long before he is old enough to use one safely! Rather than suffer the

Pictorial wallpaper, featuring plenty of action, will have enduring appeal for a little boy.

expense of a cot, then an interim first bed, it can make better sense to invest in a cotbed then, when your little boy reaches five, he can move straight to the lower level of a bunk bed that will last him to the teenage years. If he does move from a cot to a bed, then a built-in bed – at a suitably low level – or a sleigh bed is a safe and cosy choice.

Remaining furniture should be chosen with practicality and fun in mind, but it must also be safe. Once little boys can walk, they can also climb. Anticipate potential hazards by choosing sturdy pieces that can't be tipped up. For example, a solid chest of drawers with a changing mat on top is better than a changing table with open shelves, as they will

left **In a tiny attic nursery, a wall devoted to built-in shelves and cupboards creates a tranquil, modern look. If you're planning and building while your baby is still in a cot, decide in advance where a first bed will go.**

become a tempting mountain to scale. Furniture on castors can be wheeled around for fun, but is practical (for you) for manoeuvring with one hand at the baby stage, too. Tall, thin items, such as a bookshelf, should be securely fixed to the wall. Choose a low chair, so little boys aren't tempted to climb up and over the other side. A giant bean bag is an alternative, as are big floor cushions.

It may seem sexist, but little boys really don't need a proper wardrobe. Tiny jeans and T-shirts are best in a chest of drawers or stacked in a painted steel locker-style cabinet. When choosing storage for a toddler, make sure drawers glide open easily, and that they are not too deep, otherwise clothes get muddled. Long, thin D-handles, chunky knobs or cut-out apertures are all easy for chubby hands to grasp later on. Go low, so tinies can access all the drawers. Wall hooks are great for a dressing gown or fleece. If your son has a really tiny bedroom, look out for cot and bed styles with drawers underneath. Or invest in canvas storage containers to hold toys and shoes.

Add a built-in niche for necessities like a cup or books.

left and opposite, below
For a streamlined environment, clutter must be kept at bay. Here, toys are easy to access, yet simple to put away in under-bed storage, and a wall-mounted light and niche means there's no need for a bedside table.

Antique children's beds often come in comfortingly tiny proportions, so can make an ideal choice for a first bed once a child graduates from his cot.

Aim for a nursery layout that frees up as much floor space as possible. This means there's more room for a baby to crawl about or play, and less chance of you (or him) tripping over pieces of furniture. It's always cosier for a cot or first bed to be aligned against one wall, or tucked into a corner. You might even consider devoting an entire wall to a built-in wardrobe, storage unit and flip-down changing zone. Always provide a bookshelf, because every baby amasses a multitude of books from day one. Fix it very low down, so your little one can help himself to favourite volumes, or gather books into a shallow basket to tuck under the cot.

Decoratively speaking, it's important to concentrate on creating a characterful scheme that your baby will grow up to enjoy, rather than a cleverly put together themed bedroom. Save that for older children, who will get more fun out of it. In these early years, concentrate on eye-catching shades and cheerful motifs. Colours that make you feel uplifted will please your baby, too. White, teamed with splashes of citrus such as lime or tangerine, is fun and modern; consider white walls with a brightly coloured wool carpet. For a more traditional mood, by all means choose blue, but choose a variation on the palette. Pale-blue chalky walls look fantastic with accents of scarlet and natural wood, or a true denim blue, used for upholstery, looks fresh with white-painted panelling.

If you are longing to use patterned wallpaper – and there are now many charming designs on the market, from lighthouses to starships – then it looks more modern to use it just on one wall. Pick out one of the chief colours, then use it as a contrasting paint shade on the remaining walls. More unusually, you could wallpaper the ceiling: babies spend a lot of time on their backs, so deserve something interesting to look at. If you want less pattern, scrutinize fabric ranges for a memorable textile, which may be made up into a Roman blind or used to upholster a nursery armchair.

left **If you don't want
pastels, deep tones like
purple or navy, or
splashes of a bright
primary colour such as
red, can still be suitable
for little boys' rooms.
The trick is to mix strong
colours with pale tones
to keep things fresh. In
this little boy's room, a
panel of bold scarlet is
combined with white
walls and painted
floorboards, so it
doesn't look too
overpowering.**

above left **A little boy
doesn't necessarily need
a proper bedside table,
complete with electric
lamp, just because he
has moved into a bed.
But a tiny table, with
room for a cup and some
favourite books, can be
a useful extra.**

above right **Shelves can
be used to display
favourite baby toys and
special gifts in the early
years, then gradually
filled with books as your
little boy grows.**

far left **If a cot or bed is placed directly beneath a window, plan window treatments sensibly. You'll need a blackout blind or well-fitting shutters to keep out the light. Choose simple window treatments for little boys. A crisp, tailored Roman blind in denim, cotton or a ticking stripe is an excellent choice, as are American-style shutters. For safety's sake, keep blind cords short.**

left and opposite **Give due importance to a little boy's treasured collection of soft toys, from teddies to hand-knitted presents from Granny. Don't overload the bed: cluster a few favourites on the pillow and tuck the rest into a bedside basket or trunk.**

A mix of antique furniture, plus some painted junk-shop finds, makes a relaxed and sensible choice for energetic little boys.

Funky bedding ranges, teamed with plain walls, are another rich source of fun nursery motifs. Don't overdo the pattern. In a little boy's room, ticking stripes, bold gingham or big checks are great coordinates to mix in.

Finally, don't forget the tactile factor. Tiny boys, just like little girls, love to snuggle up in soft, warming textures,

and it's up to you to provide plenty of cocooning fabrics. There's plenty of time, later on, for rough, tough canvas and denim. Treat your little boy to a fleecy blanket on the bed, a thick rug to play on – a target, alphabet or modern stripe design always looks good – and he will grow up feeling that his bedroom is a safe, comforting place to be.

Stripes and checks, in shades of blue or red, are a classic and attractive combination for boys.

Whether twins will be sharing a room, or you're moving a baby in with a toddler sibling, careful planning will ensure a good night's sleep for them both. It's fun to share, but little people often have varying sleep patterns, not to mention the need for a private space all of their own. Plenty of storage – so it's easy to tidy, and peaceful at night – is the key.

SHARED ROOMS

right **In this attic bedroom for two little girls, there's little space for free-standing furniture. To keep the look uncluttered, high bedsteads provide an area beneath for storing out-of-season clothes, while a built-in cupboard at the opposite end of the room utilizes under-eaves space. If there's room on a landing just outside a shared room, this can be a good spot for a chest of drawers or a proper wardrobe.** *below* **Little children don't need a bedside light, and they're easily knocked over. In this traditional bedroom, a vintage wall sconce looks nostalgic, and provides a soft glow.**

right **Novelty clothes pegs, either in a Shaker-style painted wood design or in metal with jolly motifs, are always a winner with little ones. Hang them low on the wall, so they can reach their own clothes, and learn to tidy up.**

For most parents, the issue of sharing won't arise until baby number two (or three!) is on the way, and it's apparent that there are no more spare bedrooms. If there are twins due, a shared space is essential from day one. Those who find it tricky to get an overexcited child off to sleep may be horror-struck at the prospect of a new baby joining the fray, but careful planning can work wonders. Well-arranged space, with tranquil decoration, goes a long way towards calmer bedtimes.

If a bedroom is too small, neither child has enough personal space. So evaluate whether the room you've chosen can cope, not just with two cots or beds, but double the number

of possessions. Draw up a floor plan, with to-scale drawings of furniture, and move them around to find the most streamlined arrangement. Review all available bedrooms: does it make more sense, for example, for you to devote the master bedroom to a shared bedroom/playroom, while you create a new parents' suite in a loft extension? Might two tiny rooms be knocked into one? If you have only two bedrooms but three children, don't necessarily allocate the single room to the oldest child or the baby. Let the lightest sleeper have the room of his or her own.

Moving a new baby into an older child's bedroom must be approached with sensitivity. Tiny children are

this page **Pep up a neutral scheme, suitable for a boy and girl sharing, using identical but contrast coloured sets of bedding. Instead of pastel pink and blue, choose shades that are acceptable to either sex, such as powder blue or raspberry red with lime detailing. To ring the changes within a tightly coordinated colour scheme, choose bedding in a mix of stripes, checks and gingham; patterns that are suitable for boys or girls.** *opposite* **For a boy and girl twin, a spacious shared armoire provides plenty of clothes storage. Inexpensive drawer units have been covered with colour-coded wallpaper, but you could also use plain paint.**

If it is big enough, design a shared room with lots of free floor space, so it can double as a play zone.

quite territorial, and won't take kindly to having their personal space cluttered with a cot and a new baby. Also, try to avoid putting your toddler into a new bed while simultaneously settling the baby into the newly vacated, much-loved cot. Make the alterations in stages, and sweeten the pill for the older child by adding new bedding or a special bedside rug.

It's important to find the right spot for each bed. If you're arranging a room with a cot and a single bed, each sleeping zone may have different criteria. If a baby wakes frequently in the night, you'll want to position the cot near to the door, so you don't disturb a sleeping toddler. In a loft room, tuck the older child's bed beneath a sloping ceiling and

Mix together each child's treasures for a colourful and varied display.

position the cot in a full-head-height area of the room, so you can comfortably see to the baby's needs. It's great to divide up a room fairly, but a baby won't notice if he or she is tucked into a corner. Let your older child have the lion's share of floor space, and a window to peep out of, too.

Twin babies, or siblings close in age, will derive comfort from being able to see each other at night, so will prefer cots or beds close to each other, either positioned in parallel or in an L-shape. In between

the two cots, place a changing table, or a low chest of drawers. Toddlers in beds will enjoy having an armchair between the beds, for bedtime stories. It's a good idea to have one wall light or low-voltage ceiling light above each bed – controlled by a different switch on a dimmer – so that if one child is sleeping, and the other is awake, you have decent illumination.

If little children share, but disturb one another, the solution may be physically screening off each sleeping zone.

opposite, left **A pinboard is an excellent home for children's artworks and treasures. Opt for a metal or cork board, or use colourful felt or a large map for a cheerful background.**

opposite, right **If you only have room for one chest of drawers in a shared room, allocate the lower drawers to the toddler, and stash away baby clothes and supplies in the upper ones.**

above **Deep open shelves that run the whole length of one wall mean that little ones can use their bedroom as a playroom, as toys, storybooks and puzzles are easy to access.**

Combine a
bedroom and
play corner for
the best use of
available space.

opposite **Although this shared little girls' bedroom has a predominantly hot pink colour scheme, the bold splashes of bright egg-yolk yellow and a multi-coloured rug ensure that the inevitable primary-coloured toys don't look out of place.**

this page **Low twin beds, well within sight of one another, make a much more sociable shared bedroom arrangement for little girls than bunk beds. The crisp pink-and-white colour scheme can easily adapt to more sophisticated accessories as the girls grow older.**

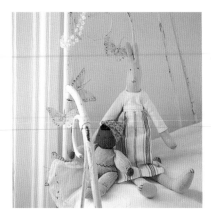

In a large room, you might divide up the space using a floor-to-ceiling storage unit, with cupboards, shelves and even a porthole to make it fun. If a baby and toddler can't physically see one another once in bed, they will settle more easily. In a modern house, sliding MDF partitions can be pushed aside by day, but transform the room into two tiny sleeping zones at night. A pretty and simple solution is to add a ceiling-hung mosquito net to both beds or cots.

Whether you choose one wardrobe, either built-in or free-standing, for the children to share, or give each child a sense of identity with their own chest of drawers, depends on the size of the room. If space is tight, it makes more sense to devote one wall to built-in cupboards. Unless children are very different in age, it's likely they will share toys and books, so combined storage is ideal. Every child, even tinies, likes to keep a few

precious things separate. Provide each one with a wall-mounted shelf near their bed or cot for treasures.

If same-sex siblings or identical twins share, it can be fun to choose a scheme suitable for an all-girl or all-boy room. A nursery with two sets of everything, from bed linen to cots, looks very cosy. If you have a baby and a toddler, search out a nursery range with a matching cot and first bed, or buy identical cotbeds. Add personality to each child's area. Hang a special painting, or a wooden initial, or choose reversible bed linen, so that each bed displays a different pattern in a common colour. Scatter cushions, a rug, or a hand-knitted blanket, in contrasting shades for each bed, also inject variety.

By contrast, when a girl and a boy share it's important to pick a decorative scheme that works for both. You may not wish to go down the pink-for-girls and blue-for-boys

left, right and below

In this large bedroom, shared by a baby boy and older sister, each has an appropriate sleeping zone on either side of the room. While the little girl has the freedom of a pretty iron bed, chest of drawers and the window, the boy's corner has been made cool and fun with vintage toys, maps and sailing memorabilia.

this page **This little boys' room has been traditionally decorated to blend with a period house yet retains a sense of fun, with hand-painted names on the door and strong blue walls. While all storage is shared – the antique armoire holds toys, with a chest of drawers for clothes – by placing the tiny beds at each side of the room, each boy has a sense of privacy. A mosquito net above each bed feels cosy when let down at night.**

route, but many accessories still come in those classic colours. So white or neutral walls, from cream to khaki, are a good choice, as you can add lilacs and reds to the girl's zone and indigo and orange to the boy's space, in the form of bedding, cushions and so on. Alternatively, choose wallpaper, curtain fabric or matching bed linen in a colour or with a motif that both little ones will enjoy. If you want colour on the walls, certain shades suit both sexes. Sherbet yellow, azure, warm apricot and leaf green are all jolly choices.

Babies and children have little personalities from birth. In a shared room, it's vital to celebrate their individuality by showing off treasured possessions. So provide a pinboard close to each child's bed for postcards, photos and artworks. Even little ones like to distinguish whether their, or their sibling's, area is a girl's, or a boy's, zone. Flags, aeroplanes, chunky furniture and cheerful colours will delineate a boy's territory, while fairies, butterflies, pastels and flowers are instant code for a girl's special patch.

above, left to right **Even tiny children will soon start to recognize the significance of their own name or their initials. Individualize two identical beds by providing a personalized blanket for each child, hand-painting their name on the bedhead, or adding a named toy close to the bed.**

BATHROOMS

All a baby really needs for bathing is a plastic bath and soft towels, so clear a space in the main bathroom for toiletries and bath toys. Toddlers, by contrast, require splashproof surfaces and lots of room to have fun, so plan for that. Create a welcoming and efficient family bathroom, with plenty of storage and safety features for little people, and you'll find the effort is well worth the investment.

right **This modern bathroom in a loft extension proves that with streamlined sanitaryware you can tuck a kids' bathroom into a tiny space. The deep bath makes bathtime fun for little children. When insetting a bath into a tiled surround, add a deep shelf around the perimeter for toys and toiletries. Have fun choosing towels and (below) flannels. You don't have to select cartoon-emblazoned styles: instead go for strong colours, abstract patterns or softer pastel shades. Beach towels offer good choices.**

A compact attic bathroom is perfect for little ones.

above **Even tiny babies need a starter kit for grooming. Include a hairbrush, toothbrush, nail scissors, cotton wool and baby massage oils. Choose a lockable cabinet to store a thermometer, medicine and other basics.**

For a new parent, having a tiny, slippery crying infant to undress and bathe can be horribly stressful. Later on, children's bathtime becomes one of the best bits of the day, a time to have fun and chat, as well as get clean. So check now whether your existing facilities will work effectively with little ones around.

In an ideal world, most parents would prefer to have a grown-up en-suite bath or shower room, and another bathroom for children and guests. If there is only one small bathroom, could it be made bigger, perhaps by stealing space from an adjacent bedroom? A growing family will reap the benefit of more space, perhaps allowing for twin basins or

a shower. If you have a spare bedroom, or are planning a loft extension and can install a new one, it's well worth creating a children's bathroom.

In the early days, you need little for bathing baby. A traditional plastic or bucket-style baby bath is essential. Some baths come with stands or fit across the top of the family bath, but it makes more sense to place it on the floor. This way, you can lay out all the necessary toiletries and towels and bathe baby in a comfortable kneeling position. Pick a baby bath to match your bathroom or, if you have an all-white scheme, choose a zingy colour, with towels to match.

You'll also need a top-and-tail bowl and something to hold essentials like

Plan a family bathroom with plenty of hard-working storage for all the kids' things. An all-white scheme accessorized with jellybean colours suits everyone.

below **This cleverly designed family bathroom, with a double-ended bath tucked to one side, has lots of floor space for several kids to run around, or in which to bath baby on the floor.**

The waist-height worktop is wide enough to take a changing mat, but in later years can double as a laundry-sorting surface. Every family bathroom needs a laundry basket and a good flip-top bin.

nappy creams, baby powder and nail scissors. Many plastic baths come with a set to match, but it's more fun to choose your own. Stock up on flannels, hooded towels and bath mats, and keep all these bathtime essentials close to hand. Clear a shelf, or invest in a trolley (some baby trolleys have a changing mat on top). Store plastic bath toys in a well-ventilated laundry bin.

If you're planning a bathroom from scratch, built-in storage is a boon. In a decent-sized room, a full-height cupboard will hold everything from spare towels to the baby bath. A vanity unit-style cupboard beneath a wall-mounted basin is a good place to hide nappies or, later on, a stool for stepping up to the basin.

Little ones should look forward to bathtime, so make the room cosy. If you are doing a bathroom from scratch, install underfloor heating and a heated towel rail (position this on the wall, rather than at floor level, so little fingers don't get burnt). Flooring and walls should be waterproof, so toddlers can splash around without fuss. Mosaic, ceramic

left **Provide sturdy hooks or a heated towel rail within grabbing distance of the bath, so little ones can wrap up quickly.**

above and top **If you're on a tight budget, an all-white bathroom is a good choice, and can easily be jazzed up with colourful accessories. Bold paintings, plastic toys, or a non-slip rubber bath mat are all good additions.**

or limestone tiles are all good choices, as they can be taken up the bath surround or even the walls. Alternatively, choose lino, rubber or vinyl tiles, which come in bright colours or funky designs. Sanded and painted floorboards are an inexpensive alternative, but avoid carpet, which will just get soggy, or wood veneer flooring.

If you're choosing sanitaryware for a children's bathroom, choose a basic white style, with taps that little ones find easy to turn – levers and cross-head styles are best. A mixer tap means there's less risk of a child getting scalded. Where space is tight, choose a bath rather than a shower, as little ones prefer bathing. Many companies do baths designed for

Soothing pastels are a restful choice in a family bathroom.

left In a traditional bathroom, it's less appropriate to have brightly coloured accessories. Instead, go with the flow with pretty towels, such as these flower-sprig ones, or gingham or pastel stripes. A big basket is useful for extra towels or spare nappies.

above For little ones getting in and out, the lower the bath, the better. A small stool also helps. If you want a fabric shower curtain, then line it with a plastic inner curtain.

this page **Once toddlers can walk, they will quickly want the independence of reaching up to the basin by themselves. Help them to do this by providing a sturdy one- or two-step stool. There are attractive painted wood ones available, or you could choose a plastic one, which is light and portable. You should also provide tooth mugs, to hold baby toothpaste and brushes. Choose identical tooth mugs, each in a different colour.**

Eureka Cream

this page **Planned for baby twin girls, this bathroom is small, yet incorporates very useful storage. As well as functional cupboards beneath the twin basins, there are open shelves for extra towels, muslins and baskets for toiletries.**

Keep pills and potions out of reach in a lockable medicine cabinet.

small rooms and a sitz or corner style is guaranteed to appeal to little ones. If you are choosing a full-size bath, pick a double-ended style, so when kids are bathing together one won't get the tap end. Choose a basin that small children can use easily: a wall-mounted rectangular basin or classic pedestal style is best.

As for decoration, keep things simple. If there is just one family bathroom, create a space that is soothing for grown-ups once tinies are in bed. Plain white sanitaryware teamed with natural surfaces like stone or wood and knocked-back pastels such as blue-grey or taupey pink will provide a stylish backdrop to bright toys and towels. In children-only bathrooms, be bold with colour. A tangerine rubber floor, turquoise ceramic tiles or a funky shower curtain will make the bathroom a fun and stimulating place to be.

below, left to right

The most user-friendly bathrooms combine a mix of storage options. Built-in cupboards, hooks and wall-mounted shelves are all invaluable.

It can come as a shock to have your beautifully planned kitchen infiltrated by baby kit, from a highchair to feeding bottles. But there is a way to blend the two stylishly. Take time to research good-looking seating, equipment and eating utensils, in colours to match your kitchen, and you'll be a long way towards creating a practical and family-friendly eating area.

EATING AREAS

right **If possible, a family kitchen should be big enough to provide a cooking zone and a separate eating and play area. A vintage or rustic style, with unfitted appliances and painted cupboards, creates a relaxed, cheerful mood and easy-care surfaces for little children.**

below **Not all baby tableware has to be plastic. Antique children's cutlery, teamed with metal or wooden platters, will withstand knocks and is highly practical. However, it's important to check that cutlery doesn't have serrated edges that could cut a little mouth.**

In the early months, your baby will be exclusively breast- or bottle-fed and won't even need a highchair, but your kitchen will still require a little rearranging. If you're bottle-feeding, you will need to accommodate a sterilizer and bottles. For many of us, the kitchen becomes the playroom, so do a safety check right now. Anticipate the crawling stage by dealing with trailing wires and fitting plug covers. Find the safest place for a baby to play, well away from the hob or electrical appliances.

Once weaning starts, it won't be long before you need a highchair, although small babies still in need of support may be better off wedged into a 'babysitter' seat or a bouncy chair. Purchasing a highchair can be a thorny issue. Some styles are an eyesore and take up too much floor space. Research a chair that looks good in your kitchen. A simple wood style is your best bet. Some highchairs are designed to 'grow up' with baby, and transform into a child's seat or a mini table and chair, so can be a sound investment. Reproduction period styles are good in a country kitchen. Pick a highchair that can be drawn up to the family table, as it's lonely for a baby to eat alone.

Once a toddler can sit at the table, ensure surfaces are wipe-clean and practical. If you have upholstered chairs, have cotton loose covers made to protect them, or move them to the

above left **Duralex glassware or colourful plastic tumblers are ideal for small children, as they won't break if dropped.**
above right **A highchair helps bridge the gap before a toddler can sit on a proper dining chair.**

For the most stylish family-friendly kitchen, seek out beautifully designed kids' tableware in funky colours, but without cartoon motifs.

dining room, and buy an inexpensive set of polypropylene or wood veneer chairs. Safeguard the table top with a wipe-clean oilcloth. In a modern kitchen, a stainless-steel tabletop or a scrubbed pine kitchen table is a practical alternative.

Babies and little children do make a mess when eating, so it can be a good idea to invest in a vinyl 'splat mat', which goes directly beneath a highchair to catch any stray food. If you're planning a family kitchen from scratch, choose easy-care flooring that can be cleaned without fuss. A stone floor looks chic, is ultra practical, and can be underfloor-heated. Rubber tiles or lino add a bright splash of colour and are comfy underfoot, or opt for sanded and

opposite **Babies are sociable creatures and don't always want to be banished upstairs to their rooms during the daytime. If there's a quiet nook in the kitchen to keep a second Moses basket or a bouncy cradle, let baby nap or play there.**

this page **The secret to a streamlined family kitchen is to plan a home for everything. A breakfast bar is ideal for tucking a highchair or little scooters well out of the way. Later on, older children will enjoy perching up at the bar on tall stools.**

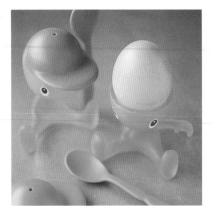

waxed or painted floorboards. Avoid
a wood veneer floor, which may
scratch easily.

It's amazing how quickly a small
child amasses a collection of cups,
cutlery and bowls. Allocate a low
cupboard to kids' tableware, then as
toddlers become independent they
can help themselves. By contrast,
once tinies are mobile, you'll need
to fit safety catches on cupboards
or drawers containing potentially
dangerous items.

It's fun to choose tableware
designed for children. Nowadays
there are trendy designs that sit very
well in a designer kitchen. If your
look is more rustic, enamel bowls,
spotty plastic plates and retro-style
pastel cutlery will look good.

A few sensible additions will
benefit most new families. Invest in
a microwave for warming bottles and
mini pureed meals, and don't forget
a stereo for nursery-rhyme CDs. Last,
but not least, a pinboard is helpful
and makes life feel organized again.

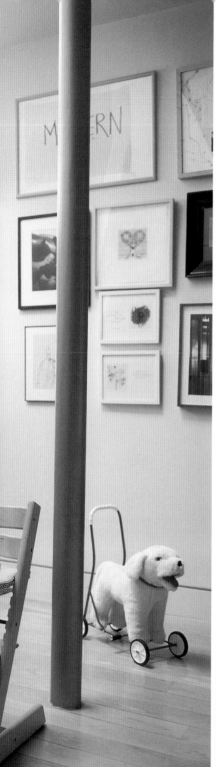

opposite, far left and centre **Look out for well-designed baby tableware that combines ease of use for little ones and good looks for you.**
main picture and below **A large table can double up as an eating zone as well as a space for little ones to draw and paint.**
left **Stylish twin high-chairs take pride of place in this slick modern kitchen.**

A tiny baby needs little more than a rattle and a soft mat in its waking hours, yet it is never too early to devise a stimulating play area. Toddlers need a place they can call their own, filled with toys and craft materials, and enough space to let off steam, so plan a safe, well-organized zone decorated with imagination and fun.

PLAY ZONES

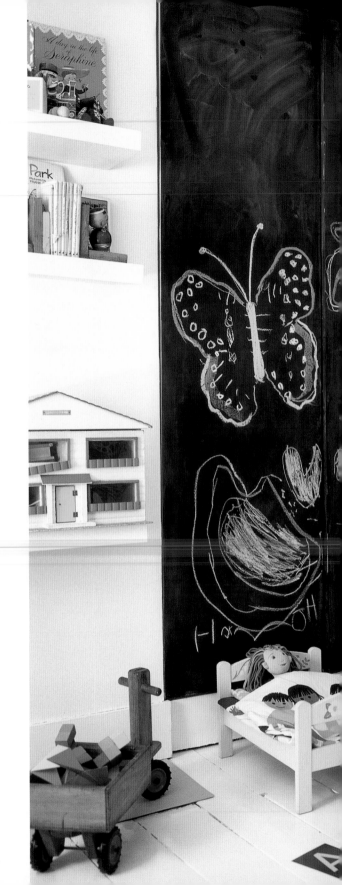

Having enough room at home for a designated playroom is probably every child's (and every parent's) dream. Toys, dolly buggies, paints and more can all be kept together in one place. Yet the reality of family life is rather different. We don't all have a spare room to devote to the children and, besides, modern living means most families prefer to congregate in the kitchen. When children are tiny, you'll also want to keep a close eye on them at all times.

Therefore it makes most sense to plan a play area within a living room or kitchen, or to look for an under-used space that may be transformed into a play zone. These days many of us have an open-plan kitchen/dining room. Is it possible to rearrange the area to create a play corner away from cooking activity? Would you get more use out of a formal dining room or study if it became a family den? If there's a generously proportioned

hall adjacent to the kitchen, or a small conservatory off the living room, it may be reinvented as a play zone. Look for spaces that can be fitted with cupboards, so toys are easily tidied away at night, which is especially important if you've taken over a portion of a busy traffic area.

First, mentally divide the area into an active zone and a chill-out corner, and decide how you will allocate the available space. This is important, because if you have busy toddlers they will need a reasonable amount of floor area for pushing toy buggies or building bricks. Yet a peaceful, safe spot is also important for a baby lying under a baby gym, and little ones in need of some downtime. By thinking through what activities will go on where, you can plan efficient storage, too.

Decoratively speaking, remember that this is an area especially for your children, so do make it fun. You will

left and opposite **For little ones, most of the action takes place on the floor: balance that decoratively with visual interest on the walls. Here, cupboards are painted with blackboard paint, so children can scrawl away, while art is hung at a higher level.**

right and below **Plan a mix of storage, from wall hooks to shelves and baskets. Units on castors are useful.**

need to tread a fine line between blending whimsical touches with the existing grown-up décor. For example, a daybed for watching DVDs might be upholstered in a cheerful modern cotton, which acts both as an accent shade in a predominantly neutral interior and looks jolly for kids. Likewise, framed colourful abstract art adds a quirky touch to the walls without the need to repaint them in a brighter tone. If sophisticated dark wood or limestone flooring is continuous with the rest of the room, adding a children's-design wool rug will bring softness and character to the new zone.

Adding scaled-down furniture is the most thoughtful way to personalize a play area for tinies. It's possible to find lovely mini table and chair sets, from colourful animal-painted designs to vintage styles,

above **If a child has a large bedroom, consider creating a play area in one corner. This can be a particularly good idea for a baby who has much older (and rowdier) siblings, and needs a quiet, cosy place to play. Add a comfortable daybed and a low table that is easy for a toddler to reach.**

left and above **A large landing makes a spacious play zone. Toys can be tucked under the stairs at night, and a simple mural, appropriate for little ones and grown-ups alike, creates a magical setting.**

A small playroom, linked to an open-plan kitchen via a sliding door, can be closed off for quiet play, or left sociably open.

so pick one that blends in at home. If a tiny table isn't big enough for several toddlers, then buy a junk-shop table, cut down its legs, paint it in a zingy colour, and accessorize with tiny stools. Low-level soft seating is a brilliant addition for children who spend a lot of time on the floor. Giant beanbags are great for babies, as they provide comfy support, and padded play mats are fun for rolling around on. Also consider seating cubes and floor cushions.

Don't forget to provide somewhere comfy for you to sit while reading stories or watching a DVD. If there is room, a two-seater sofa or a daybed is ideal. Add lots of cushions and a soft, washable throw, useful for impromptu daytime naps or just

opposite, left and right
**Once babies make the
transition to crawling
and then toddling, a
playroom must be made
safe. This pinboard is
jolly to look at, but is
positioned high up, so
little fingers can't
remove pictures or pins.**
left **Consider a low
seating unit along one
wall, fitted with floor-
level drawers. Little
ones will enjoy sitting
on top, if there are
plenty of soft cushions.**
above **Keep an easel out
on display, or cover an
expanse of wall with
blackboard paint, so
children can easily
indulge in some painting
and drawing.**

below **A play zone doesn't have to be huge to satisfy toddlers. This small conservatory, off the kitchen and leading on to the garden, provides a safe place for little ones to keep busy. In a traditional-style house, choose an antique cupboard and wicker baskets to conceal toy storage.**

right **If you don't want to compromise on a sophisticated, neutral decorative scheme, remember that toys themselves provide lots of colour and charm. In later years, this room will easily transform into a more grown-up den, with shelves for books and room for a TV and stereo.**

A play area adjacent to the kitchen is both practical and sociable.

right **One end of this little girl's bedroom has been kitted out with a tiny table and chairs and mobile book units. It's sensible to keep a sleep zone and play area separate, so a child will settle easily at night.**

snuggling under. In play areas with a TV, ensure that it is positioned low down, so you and the children can watch comfortably, but with the DVD player out of reach of toddlers.

Every play area needs great storage, so that small children can easily access toys and help tidy them away. A floor-to-ceiling shelf unit or a free-standing armoire is a good starting point. Line the shelves with baskets, boxes or crates, so bricks, Lego and jigsaws can be quickly sorted. You might want to colour-code containers, or stick a picture of each toy type on to the exterior. Small children can't read, but will quickly remember what goes where.

Choose generously proportioned containers, as babies' and toddlers' possessions are often bulky. Keep toys on low shelves, so little ones can help themselves, and store craft materials at a higher level.

Half the fun of a play area is that it is filled with the children's things, so don't be too zealous about tidying things away. Try to allocate enough floor space so that bigger items can be left out ready for the next day's play. It's also a good idea to add a few large baskets or canvas or rubber containers for soft toys. Aim for lightly organized chaos, rather than minimalist splendour, and playtime will be fun for all concerned.

STORAGE

Infants may be small, but they have a multitude of possessions. Long before a new baby arrives, review the available storage space at home and plan for the influx of baby kit. While you can never have too much storage in a family home, choose wisely. Babies are simple souls and don't need every latest gadget.

right and below **Take time to research the ideal container, from cardboard and plywood to wicker and plastic. A shallow, well-proportioned style makes it easy to find things. Pick an open-topped variety, so you're not continually removing and replacing lids.**

From the moment you pick up your first pregnancy book and read the list of baby's layette, it becomes clear that storage at home will require a radical rethink. Babies are as much part of our fashion-conscious times as adults, and have quantities of trendy tiny clothes to prove it. And that's not all. These days there's a plethora of baby kit, from all the essentials like a buggy and a highchair, to extras such as a travel cot or portable potty. Toys there will be aplenty. If you are having your first baby, it's also likely that – as your family expands – you'll need to store outgrown clothes or kit for the next sibling.

As you start to amass equipment, perhaps prior to the birth, ask yourself where everything will go. Not everything needs to go in a cupboard: the baby bath, pram, Moses basket and car seat, for example, will be in daily use. For these, it's a case of working out where they can live comfortably, without getting in the way. If space is really tight, look for fold-up or more neatly proportioned pieces. In the downstairs rooms, it can be helpful to add a new cupboard, either in the hall or the kitchen, which can hold toy storage boxes, outdoor clothes, modes of transport and so on.

above left **An office-style chest makes it easy to organize clothes. You can also buy screw-in labels, which are brilliant for labelling drawers and shelves.**
above centre **If kids share shelves or a wardrobe, code containers, with boxes or drawers in different colours.**
above right **A clothes rail needn't be wide, but do allow space at the bottom for increasingly bigger clothes.**

below **If there is a deep alcove in the bedroom, design a walk-in wardrobe concealed behind extra-wide doors. A mix of shelves, drawers and hanging rails can keep toys and clothes sorted, as well as providing space for extras like a travel cot or larger play equipment.**

This leaves remaining floor space free for play.

right **In a modern house, look out for free-standing pieces with a sleek finish, or in a bold colour, to blend with other contemporary décor. This glossy wardrobe, in a baby boy's room, will still suit when he is a teenager.**

In the early months, the most pressing issue will be organizing baby's new things. For those who haven't managed to buy a wardrobe before the birth, three giant wicker baskets are an excellent interim measure. Fill one with clothes, one with bedding, and the other with soft toys. If a single chest of drawers is the nursery storage system, choose a style with drawers in a variety of depths. The deep bottom drawer can hold bedding, the middle ones clothes, and the top ones socks, gloves and hats.

To keep things neat on open shelves, invest in plenty of baskets or boxes (preferably matching). Don't forget that the collection will grow, so buy more then you need now. Opt for a lot of smaller containers, rather than a few big ones, as this makes life easier when it comes to sorting things. Have fun selecting the baskets: there is a huge choice, from woven plastic to wood, acrylic to canvas. Wicker baskets lined with calico or gingham won't snag little garments. If you want to be really organized, label containers according to each category.

It is an investment to choose custom-built storage, but you will find it well worth the expense. In a family home, every centimetre counts, so tuck a toy cupboard beneath the stairs, add bookshelves around a doorway, or build wardrobes in a

top, left and right **For little ones, cupboards should be accessible at a low level, with grown-up items safe on an upper level.**
above **If possible, conceal the TV in a cupboard – out of sight and out of mind until DVD time.**

Choose open-topped or light, easy-to-access containers, so children can help themselves. Pick jolly designs that look good and that they will enjoy using.

left and far right, inset **Amass a wide variety of different-size containers, for every room in the house. Look for features that make life easy, such as plastic crates that stack, boxes with** handles, and small lidded shoeboxes. Check out chain stores and DIY shops, which have a good selection of trendy, cheap containers. *below* **Little ones will play with what they can** see, so ensure that there are bowls or baskets filled with favourite things on the floor within grabbing distance. Don't overfill; otherwise things will get in a muddle.

bedroom alcove. The beauty of tailor-made storage is that if you need to store bulky items, such as a travel cot or a double buggy, you can build a cupboard in just the right proportions so the item fits perfectly.

If you're adding a built-in storage system in a child's bedroom, plan for the long term. Fix shelves on an adjustable system, so they can cater for big picture books now and paperbacks later, and ensure that at least one clothing rail is at a higher level, for older children. It can be a good idea to fill one wall with a

combination of wardrobe, bookshelves, and a deep shelf at waist height. In the first few years, the latter creates a useful surface for a changing mat, and later on it will double up as a space for drawing, then a desk for homework. Built-in furniture isn't the sole preserve of modern houses. In a period home, panelled or tongue and groove doors look perfectly in keeping.

Plenty of attractive free-standing pieces of furniture can double up to hold children's kit, so it's not necessary to compromise on style.

left and above **Look out for dual-purpose buys, which act as a piece of furniture and hold toys. Plastic stools, lidded chests and play tables are excellent choices.**

In a retro household, a trendy sideboard is great for holding a TV and DVD player or, for a simple rustic mood, choose an antique toy trunk or a country armoire. Modern furniture in glossy colourful lacquer or steel finishes looks streamlined. Many pieces come in modular units, so you can build up a collection over time. Look out for styles on castors that allow maximum flexibility for altering the layout of a room as children's needs change.

It's also worth scanning children's furniture and mail-order catalogues, for clever, child-size storage options. Some pieces are decorative and fun for the bedroom, such as shelves shaped like a skateboard or castle, a combined child's bench/toy box, or a doll's-house-style open shelf unit. Other useful storage options will help to organize busy areas such as the hall. A tiered unit, with lots of mini-drawers, a low coatstand, wall hooks and a combined bench/shoe-rack unit are all brilliant ideas for storing endless gloves, coats and hats.

You will also need to store out-of-season garments, outgrown clothes for younger siblings, or sale buys baby has yet to grow into. If you can, keep these in the attic or spare room. Department stores, specialist storage shops and mail-order catalogues are a great source of clever storage solutions, from stackable crates to under-bed storage bags.

It's important to be organized, but don't overdo the tidying. A family home, after all, derives much of its personality from the colour and character of toys, first paintings and little clothes hanging from hooks. So combine order behind closed doors, with attractive displays of favourite possessions. Celebrate your children's things and relax. A family home evolves and changes every single day, so accept that and enjoy!

opposite **Children's favourite things add great charm to a room, so show them off on a mantelpiece or shelf.** *left and right* **There's an art to using wall hooks for display. Don't over-crowd, and stick to one type of item, such as clothes and accessories.** *below* **Precious items, from baby shoes to soft toys, should be framed in glass-fronted cases to keep off dust.**

Use the prettiest clothes and accessories to make a decorative display.

CHECKLISTS

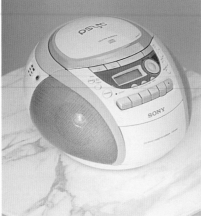

Room planning

- Is the potential bedroom big enough to accommodate the basics of a cot, changing table and feeding chair?

- Do alcoves or spare wall space allow for built-in shelves, a wardrobe or a custom-made changing table?

- Does the bedroom overlook a noisy street and, if so, can you add double glazing?

- Is the room close to the master bedroom, for easy access at night?

Furniture basics

- Moses basket or crib.

- Cot or cotbed.

- Chest of drawers with changing mat, or changing unit.

- Armchair for feeding.

- Bean bags, soft seating cubes or floor cushions.

- Wall-mounted shelves or a built-in bookcase.

- Wall hooks and hangers, or wardrobe with hanging rail.

Essentials to store in the bedroom

- The changing mat, wipes, nappies, creams, cotton wool and muslin squares.

- Clothing, including vests, sleepsuits, tops and trousers, jumpers, hats, coats, socks and bootees.

- Changing bag for outings.

- Baby rattles, soft toys, baby board books.

- Bedding, including fitted cot sheets, top sheets, cellular or fleece blankets, a cotton quilt, or baby sleeping bags.

- Gifts and christening presents, including baby clothes waiting to be grown into.

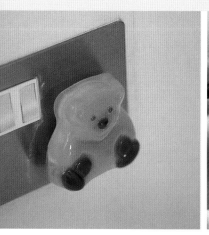

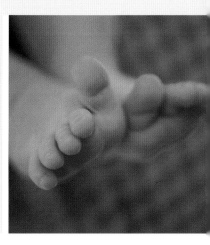

Equipment to store elsewhere

- Infant carrier car seat.

- Pram, pushchair or three-wheeler buggy.

- Baby sling and/or baby backpack carrier.

- Travel cot.

- Highchair and/or travel booster seat.

- Bouncing cradle and/or baby exerciser.

- Baby bath, toiletries and bath support.

- Bottles, bottle sterilizer, feeding bowls and spoons, bibs.

Essential toy storage

- Rubber tubs, wicker baskets or canvas containers for loose toys.

- Wall hooks for hanging fabric bags or over-door organizers for soft toys.

- Shelves for books and baskets.

- Space for fabric playhouse or tent, and sit-on cars, buggies and trikes.

- Toy boxes or crates on wheels for large cars, trains or building blocks.

- Ottoman or toy chest for baby play nest and/or baby gym.

Safety issues to consider

- Fit plastic socket covers to all electricity sockets.

- Add kitchen cabinet locks and window locks.

- Fit stair gates at the top and/or bottom of stairs.

- Wall-mount a lockable medicine cabinet in the bathroom.

- Tuck trailing wires and blind cords well out of the way.

- Buy a fire guard, but never leave a child near an open fire.

QUESTIONS & ANSWERS

Q: How can I make my baby's room safe?

A: Invest in a new cot, rather than an antique one, and check that it adheres to the correct British Standards guides. It is also recommended that every new baby have a new mattress. This should fit snugly into the cot or Moses basket, with a maximum gap of 4cm (1½in). It is never too early to fit plastic covers on every electricity socket, so that you're not caught out if baby starts crawling early. If your little one's cot is close to the window, ensure blind cords are short and kept well out of the way. For extra safety, fit window catches.

Q: Any good ideas for instant storage?

A: Make the most of hanging options, which are decorative and comparatively inexpensive. Fabric pocket tidies, which can be hung on the back of the door or from hooks, are brilliant for storing tiny items such as socks and bootees, or baby grooming items. Large laundry bags are great for hiding away spare nappies or sleepsuits. A fabric cot tidy, which ties directly on to the cot side, is useful for stashing away extra soft toys and keeping dummies to hand.

Q: Should I introduce ambient lighting?

A: It is always a good idea to add a dimmer switch to the overhead light, so you can settle baby easily. But it's also fun to introduce a secondary light source, as an amusement for your baby, or to provide extra illumination on dark days or for night-time visits. A conventional lamp, with a pretty lampshade, creates a gentle pool of light, but must be located well out of grabbing distance of the cot. For a funkier look, consider a string of fairy lights, an LED wall panel, or a revolving magic lantern to cast gentle patterns on the wall. A plug-in nightlight with a pretty motif also provides a comforting glow.

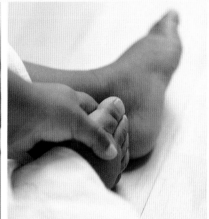

Q: Are there any stylish alternatives to curtains with blackout lining?

A: If you're after a clean, simple look, then blinds or shutters are good-looking and highly practical. In a period property with sash windows, consider commissioning a carpenter to build new wooden shutters, which are brilliant for keeping out daylight. American-style shutters with adjustable slats, or Venetian blinds, will let in as much, or as little, light as you wish – good for waking up a baby gently. Mail-order blind specialists offer a wide variety of roller and Roman blinds in everything from denim to feather-emblazoned styles.

Q: Do I really have to have a character-emblazoned plastic changing mat?

A: There are stylish alternatives! If you have a simple, modern scheme, then look for a foam-filled mat in white, or a plain pastel colour. Increasingly, it's possible to buy comfortable wedge-shape changing mats that come with a removable fabric cover, in chic variations from waffle cotton to pretty gingham edging, or plain white towelling.

Q: What can I add to stimulate baby?

A: Even tiny babies will appreciate movement and sound to stimulate them while they lie in the cot. Attractive options to try include stringing gingham bunting across the ceiling, or hanging a paper mobile where it will twirl in the breeze, or individual colourful glass chandelier droplets, securely hung to catch the light. A windchime can also be a charming addition. Make sure there are enough soft toys in the cot for baby to play with (ensure they are suitable for babies), and add a wind-up musical mobile. Later on, a cot activity centre is fun. It may not be a thing of beauty, but your baby will love it.

HIGH-STREET FURNITURE

Argos
Call 0870 600 1010 or visit
www.argos.co.uk for details of your
nearest store.
Nursery furniture, toy boxes and seating.

Ikea
Call 0845 355 1141 or visit
www.ikea.co.uk for details of your
nearest store.
*Trendy kids furniture: cots, extendable
beds, storage and funky accessories.*

John Lewis
Call 0845 604 9049 or visit
www.johnlewis.com for details of your
nearest store.
*Moses baskets, cribs, cots and cotbeds,
changing tables and furniture.*

Lullabys
01743 367 994
www.lullabys.co.uk
Cots, highchairs and accessories.

Marks & Spencer
Call 0845 603 1 603 or visit
www.marksandspencer.com for details
of your nearest store.
*Iron, wicker and wood children's beds,
plus bedding and basic storage.*

Mothercare
Call 0845 330 4030 or visit
www.mothercare.com for details of your
nearest store.
*Modern and traditional furniture ranges,
plus accessories and equipment.*

DESIGNER FURNITURE

Chic Shack
77 Lower Richmond Road
London SW15 1ET
020 8785 7777
www.chicshack.net
*White-painted furniture in traditional
styles. Cots and cotbeds, storage,
changing tables and wardrobes.*

The Children's Furniture Company
Call 020 7737 7303 or visit
www.thechildrensfurniturecompany.com
*Single beds with matching wardrobes,
chests of drawers and toy boxes in
hardwoods, with interchangeable
colour panels.*

Daisy and Tom
181–183 Kings Road
London SW3 5EB
020 7349 5800
www.daisyandtom.com
*Attractive selection of brand-name cots,
pushchairs, nursery furniture and
bedding, plus accessories and lighting.*

Lionwitchwardrobe
Call 020 8318 2070 or visit
www.lionwitchwardrobe.co.uk
*Solid maple and oak beautifully crafted
cots and cotbeds, cot-top changing
units, and wardrobes, plus a bespoke
furniture service.*

Simon Horn
117–121 Wandsworth Bridge Road
London SW6 2TP
020 7731 1279
www.simonhorn.com
*Beautifully made lit bateau cotbeds, plus
matching chest of drawers and wardrobe
designed to grow with your child.*

The Swedish Chair
48 Heathhurst Road
Sanderstead
Surrey CR2 0BA (by appointment only)
020 8657 8560
www.theswedishchair.com
*Adorable painted Swedish-style furniture,
featuring traditional highchair, cot,
extendable bed and clothes peg rails.*

Stokke UK
Call 01753 655 873 or visit
www.stokke.com for details of your
nearest retailer.
*Quality modern Scandinavian furniture
including a cot, changing table and high
chair, all designed to grow with your child.*

MAIL ORDER

Aspace
01985 301 222
www.aspaceuk.com
*Specialist children's furniture company
with simply designed cots, cotbeds, first
and single size beds, plus good storage,
accessories and lighting.*

Blooming Marvellous
0845 458 7408
www.bloomingmarvellous.co.uk
*Comprehensive range of nursery
furniture, including rocking cribs, cots,
storage and prettily styled accessories.*

Bump
020 7249 7000
www.bumpstuff.com
*Flat-pack MDF nursery and single bed
size beds, with Swedish styling, ready to
paint in your own colours.*

The Great Little Trading Company
0870 850 6000
www.gltc.co.uk
*Excellent range of children's furniture,
including storage, safety gadgets, bed
linen and eating accessories.*

JoJo Maman Baby
0870 241 0451
www.jojomamanbebe.co.uk
*Cribs and cots, great storage, plus
bedding, nightlights and accessories.*

The Little White Company
261 Pavilion Road
London SW1X 0BP
0870 900 9555
www.thewhitecompany.com
*Classic white furniture including cots,
cotbeds, first beds and matching furniture.
Also towels, bed linens and storage.*

Next Home
0845 600 7000
www.next.co.uk
*Coordinated nursery bedding, storage
and personalized photo canvas service.*

Wigwamkids
0870 902 7500
www.wigwamkids.co.uk
*Fabulous range of nursery and children's
furniture, plus trendy accessories, bed
linen and rugs.*

BEDLINEN

Brora
344 Kings Road
London SW3 5UR
020 7736 9944
www.brora.co.uk
*Lambswool and cashmere baby blankets
in pastels, checks and stripes, plus
knitted teddies.*

Descamps
197 Sloane Street
London SW1X 9QX
020 7235 7165
www.descamps.com
*Very chic nursery and children's baby
linens, matching towels and soft toys.*

Laura Ashley
0871 230 2301
www.lauraashley.com
*Coordinated bed linen and accessories for
boys and girls, with motifs from cowboys
to flowers, and good storage boxes.*

STORAGE

The Holding Company
241–245 Kings Road
London SW3 5EL
020 8445 2888
www.theholdingcompany.co.uk
*Huge selection of every type of storage,
from seagrass baskets to children's toy
bins and cardboard storage boxes.*

Muji
41 Carnaby Street
London W1V 1PD
Call 020 7323 2208 or visit
www.muji.co.uk for details of your
nearest store.
Storage boxes, trolleys and baby toys.

STOCKISTS & SUPPLIERS

Oka Direct
The Coachworks
80 Parsons Green Lane
London SW6 4HU
0870 160 6002
www.okadirect.com
Chic rattan boxes of every size, storage trunks, bookshelves and armoires.

ACCESSORIES

Anthropology
0870 011 0511
www.anthropologygifts.com
Personalized bunting, cushions, bed linen, wall canvas pictures and bathrobes.

Cath Kidston
51 Marylebone High Street
London W1U 5HW
020 7229 8000
www.cathkidston.co.uk
Beanbags, oilcloths, towels, wallpaper and storage bags in florals, spots and retro prints.

Childhood Interiors
0870 609 2691
www.childhoodinteriors.co.uk
Contemporary children's bed linen, cheery pouffes and storage boxes.

Couverture
310 Kings Road
London SW3 5UH
020 7795 1200
www.couverture.co.uk
Vintage and traditional toys.

Ede & Nia
020 7602 8229
www.edeandnia.co.uk
Blankets, rattles and baby bootees.

E-Niko
01768 210 121
www.e-niko.co.uk
Bright nursery accessories.

JeeWhizz Designs
01949 844 481
www.jeewhizzdesigns.com
Children's play screens, plus blackboards and play tables.

Letterbox
0870 600 7878
www.letterbox.co.uk
Toys and accessories, with useful personalizing service.

Made
020 8960 6969
www.made.co.uk
Sheepskin rugs and beanbags, and rugs with target or Union Jack motifs.

Urchin
0870 720 0709
www.urchin.co.uk
Trendy baby equipment, including cribs, feeding accessories and bedding.

White Rabbit England
01625 251 188
www.whiterabbitengland.com
Charming traditional night lights, china breakfast sets and cashmere blankets.

Win Green
01622 746 516
www.wingreen.co.uk
Tents and play houses, beanbags and bunting, all in pastel gingham.

Woolworths
Call 01706 862 789 or visit www.woolworths.co.uk for details of your nearest store.
Children's bed linen and storage.

WINDOW TREATMENTS

Baer and Ingram
Dragon Works
Leigh on Mendip
Radstock
Somerset BA3 5QZ
01373 813 800
www.baer-ingram.co.uk
Made-to-order blinds, curtains and quilts.

Eclectics
Call 01843 608 789 or visit www.eclectics.co.uk for details of your nearest retailer.
Roman and roller blinds, including blackout options.

Pret a Vivre
The Curtain Room
Shelton Lodge
Shelton, Newark
Nottinghamshire NG23 5JJ
0845 130 5161
www.pretavivre.com
Made-to-order curtains and blinds, including a choice of blackout options.

The New England Shutter Company
020 8675 1099
www.tnesc.co.uk
Solid wood American-style shutters.

FABRICS & WALLPAPERS

Anna French
343 Kings Road
London SW3 5ES
020 7349 1099
www.annafrench.co.uk
Nursery fabrics and wallpapers, with classic teddy and fairy motifs.

Designers Guild
267–271 Kings Road
London SW3 5EN
020 7351 5775
www.designersguild.com
Bright and jolly fabrics and wallpapers, plus matching accessories.

Graham & Brown
0800 328 8452
www.grahambrown.com
Bright and funky wallpapers.

Jane Churchill
110 Fulham Road
London SW3 6HU
020 8877 6400
www.janechurchill.com
Children's wallpapers and fabrics, with sail boats, cowboys and little girl motifs, plus checks and dots.

Voyage Decoration
0141 641 1700
www.voyagedecoration.com
Large range of charming fabrics.

All photography by Winfried Heinze

Key: a=above, b=below, r=right, l=left, c=centre

PICTURE CREDITS

Architects and designers whose work is featured in this book:

Blue Bench
159 Duane Street
New York, NY 10013
USA
t: +1 212 267 1500
www.bluebenchnyc.com
pages 5ar, 86, 95a, 100r–101ar

Casa Kids
Roberto Gil
106 Ferris Street
Brooklyn, NY 11231
USA
t. +1 718 694 0272
www.casakids.com
pages 105r, 127

Cherner Design
Architecture & furniture design
(including 'Cherner chair')
Ben Cherner, Principal
t. +1 212 375 8464
bc@chernerdesign.com
www.chernerchair.com
pages 44–45, 101br, 103r

Emma Cassi
Lace jewellery designer
t.020 8487 2836
www.emmacassi.com
pages 22–23

Grosfeld Architecten
Pascal Grosfeld
Minervum 7489
4817 ZP Breda
The Netherlands
t. +31 76 522 18 11
www.grosfeld-architecten.nl
*pages 12–13, 18r–19l, 52–53,
76–77, 88–89, 110r, 113, 120l*

Henri Fitzwilliam-Lay Ltd
m. 07968 948 053
hfitz@hotmail.com
pages 72-3, 81b, 82r, 83l, 87bl, 112al

homity
t. 01273 672 585
www.homity.co.uk
pages 64–65, 68–69, 84l, 85, 109c

i29 design
Industrieweg 29
1115 AD Duivendrecht
The Netherlands
t. +31 20 695 61 20
www.i29.nl
pages 20–21, 28–29, 111al

Josephine Ryan Antiques
63 Abbeville Road
London SW4 9JW
t/f. 020 8675 3900
www.josephineryanantiques.co.uk
*pages 1, 5b, 36–37, 60–61, 90,
104l*

Katie Lydon Interiors
New York, NY
USA
t. +1 212 226 2690
e. kalershankey@aol.com
pages 38–39

Kid's Digs
212 West 79th Street, Apt 1-C
New York, NY 10024
USA
t. +1 212 787 7800
page 110l

Malin Iovino Design
43 St Saviour's Wharf
Mill Street
London SE1 2BE
t. 020 7252 3542
e. iovino@btconnect.com
pages 14, 16l, 18l, 58–59

Pamplemousse Design Inc
New York, USA
t. +1 212 980 2033
pages 40–41, 42–43, 100l

Silence
Creative research design
consultancy
t. 01273 299 231
www.silence.co.uk
pages 98r–99l, 112ar, 128

Studio Azzurro Architects
Chris & Milla Gough-Willetts,
Directors
t. 020 7373 2429
t. +1 415 435 5767
www.studioazzurro.co.uk
pages 30–31, 111ar, 121r

Studio Sofield
Emma O'Neill, Vice President
t: +1 212 473 1300
www.studiosofield.com
pages 44–45, 101br, 103r

**The New England Shutter
Company**
Sophie Eadie
16 Jaggard Way
London SW12 8UB
t. 0208 675 1099
www.tnesc.co.uk
*pages 5al, 34–35, 48–49, 63, 91,
112b*

Wells Mackereth Architects
5e Shepherd Street
Mayfair
London W1J 7HP
t. 020 7495 7055
www.wellsmackereth.com
*pages 70–71, 80r, 83ar, 94r–95b,
102–103l*

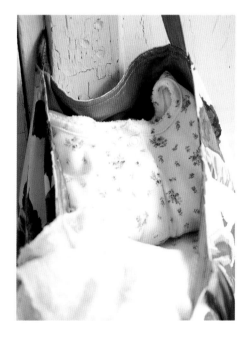

INDEX

Figures in italics indicate captions.